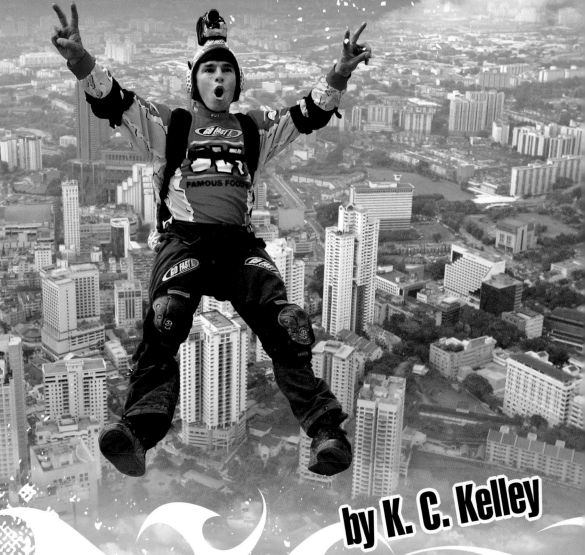

BASE Jumping

by K. C. Kelley

Published by The Child's World®
1980 Lookout Drive
Mankato, MN 56003-1705
800-599-READ
www.childsworld.com

The Child's World®: Mary Berendes, Publishing Director
Shoreline Publishing Group, LLC: James Buckley Jr.,
  Production Director
The Design Lab: Design and production

ISBN: 978-1-60973-205-9
LCCN: 2011928879

Photo credits: Cover: AP/Wide World.
Interior: Alamy: 29; AP/Wide World: 8, 11, 16; Corbis:
4, 12; dreamstime.com: Rene Drouyer: 25, Shariff Che
Lah: 15; iStock: 7, 19, 21, 22, 26.

Printed in the United States of America
Mankato, Minnesota
July, 2011
PA02094

Table of Contents

Omar Al Hegelan heads toward the ground while making the highest BASE jump ever.

CHAPTER ONE

A Long Way Down!

The tallest building in the world rises more than 2,200 feet (672 m) above the city of Dubai. Known as the Burj Khalifa, it is almost twice as high as the Empire State Building. A stack of four Washington Monuments is just barely as tall.

In January 2010, Nasser Al Neyadi jumped off the world's tallest building!

He **plummeted** toward the ground at nearly 100 miles per hour (160 kph). The hard sidewalks below zoomed toward him. Amazed people watched from the building's windows as he zipped past them.

After free-falling for several seconds, he suddenly popped his special parachute. A bloom of black nylon filled the sky over his head. His speed slowed. As crowds of people watched, he floated to a safe landing.

Even as he had plunged off the platform, Al Neyadi thought, "This is crazy." He was not alone in thinking that. Most people would never think of leaping off such a tall building, even with a parachute. BASE jumpers are not like ordinary people.

Al Neyadi and his jumping partner, Omar Al Hegelan, are part of one of the most daring of all the extreme sports: BASE jumping. BASE jumping is skydiving . . . but without an aircraft. In fact, the letters in its name stand for the places that BASE jumpers leap from:

B: building

A: antennas (very tall radio and TV masts)

S: span (this is usually a bridge)

E: earth (mountains, cliffs, high bluffs, etc.)

Here's the view from high atop an antenna.
This is one of of the four parts of BASE.

BASE jumpers made El Capitan one of their first stops.

BASE jumping started in the late 1970s when skydivers searched for new thrills. Jumping out of airplanes wasn't wild enough for them. So, naturally, they looked up. They saw tall buildings and high mountains. The jumpers wondered why they couldn't jump off things that high instead of waiting for an airplane to take them up.

The first well-known BASE jumps took place off 3,000-foot (910-m) El Capitan in California's Yosemite National Park. Carl Boenish led a group that leaped on August 18, 1978. They all made it safely and the new sport really took off. Soon, daring jumpers started stepping off high bridges over rivers. They climbed difficult cliffs . . . and then leaped off. They scaled radio antennas that looked like giant ladders . . . and jumped.

First BASE?
The El Capitan jumpers made BASE jumping well-known. They were not the first to jump off tall things, though. Since parachutes were invented in the early 1900s, people tried jumping from bridges or towers. **Daredevils** leaped off the Statue of Liberty in the 1930s and out of hot-air balloons. The key to BASE jumping in recent years was the newer parachutes. Read more about them in Chapter Two.

BASE jumpers are very careful about safety. They double-check and triple-check their gear before they jump. It is a very dangerous sport and several people have been killed or badly hurt. This is NOT a sport for just anyone to try. But for brave and skilled skydivers, BASE jumping has become a big part of their search for big thrills.

In that search, they have to overcome fear, of course. Jumping from a high place is not a natural thing for people to do. However, it can also be illegal. The first BASE jumpers had to sneak into buildings or onto bridges. Police and other people didn't want the jumpers to hurt themselves or others. Once jumpers landed after jumping off a building, they needed a getaway car to slip away before they were caught. BASE jumping had a **reputation** as a sport for sneaky—though very brave—people. As more people came to the sport, that changed.

Group jump! Three experts leap together from this building in China.

After their record-setting jump in Dubai, the two brave leapers met some fans.

Over time, however, it has become another extreme sport. Yosemite Park officials tried to stop those early jumpers in the late 1970s. They gave some jumpers permission for a while. Today, however, any BASE jumping in national parks is illegal. Many BASE jumpers do work with government or building officials to plan safer jumps. Al Neyadi, for instance, had approval from Burj Khalifa owners for his jump. BASE jumpers also use video and photos to show off their daring, too. Clips of the jumps are all over the Internet.

Many people are afraid of heights. BASE jumpers go looking for high places . . . and then they come down—fast!

CHAPTER TWO

Jumping Gear and Skills

It all starts with the parachute. BASE jumpers do not use a classic round parachute. That was the shape of chutes from when they were invented in the 1700s. The shape is still used by some skydivers. BASE jumpers and most sport skydivers now use "ram-air" parachutes. These look much more like a bird's wing than the top half of a balloon. They are rectangular and have handles that the jumper can use to steer. Air flows through pockets in the ram-air chutes so the jumpers are gliding rather than just falling.

It's no surprise that a BASE jumper's parachute must open very quickly. To help make this happen, they use a pilot chute. They toss this smaller chute—attached to the pack—soon after the jump begins. It catches the air. The force of the pilot chute then pulls

The ram-air parachute opens quickly and can be steered by the jumper.

Why Helmets?

BASE jumpers should wear helmets for each jump. It's not for protection in case their chute fails. If that happens, a helmet won't help. The helmet is used in case the jumper swings into the cliff, tower, or building while hanging under the chute. The helmet can also protect the wearer in case of a rough landing.

Safety first: Jumpers take their time to pack chutes carefully.

the larger main chute out with a rush and a pop. Remember BASE jumps last very little time. Without the pilot chute, there might not be enough time for the main chute to come out quickly without the pilot's help.

Aircraft skydivers and BASE jumpers have one big difference in their gear. Skydivers have a backup chute. If the main chute doesn't open, the jumper has time to open a second chute he or she is wearing. They are jumping from as much as 10 times higher than a BASE jumper. If a BASE jumper's chute doesn't open . . . there's no time for anything but a **fatal** landing.

That's the reason that BASE jumpers take extreme care in packing their chutes. A jumper might take 30 minutes or more to pack the chute. They might repack it several times until they are sure it's perfect. There are no mistakes allowed in BASE jumping.

With all the gear assembled, the BASE jump itself has several parts. First, the jumper must make it to the top of what he or she is jumping from. For a bridge, it's not too hard—just walk out there. To jump from buildings, they might have to climb stairs or find an elevator to the roof. Climbing huge radio antennas is usually against the rules, but some do it anyway. These towers can be dangerous, with electric shocks a possibility. For the "Earth" part of BASE, climbers might have to make long hikes, climb mountains, or carry their packs for several hours to reach the top.

Once they've reached their jump point, they test the wind. If the wind is blowing too strongly toward them, it might push them into the building or cliff wall. From the top of buildings, some jumpers drop a weighted ribbon. As it falls, the jumpers watch how the wind makes the ribbon move.

Jumpers look before leaping to make sure it's safe below.

BASE jumpers also have to make sure they have a good, safe landing area. They don't want to land in traffic or in water or on a rocky slope. So from their **lofty** height, they look down and pick a spot to aim for.

Then, with all that done, it's time to leap out as far as possible . . . and fall.

A few seconds later, they throw out the pilot chute that releases the main chute. Whew . . . it worked again!

With the ram-air chutes, BASE jumpers can steer easily toward the landing site. These chutes are designed to let the jumpers land as easily as if they have stepped off a curb.

Then it's back to packing their chute for another BASE jump!

After a soft landing, jumpers gather up their chutes.

Leaping from cliffs like this one is for experts only.

CHAPTER THREE

Stars and Records

If you're a BASE jumper, you want to find the highest thing you can find . . . and jump off it. Some jumpers aim for records that will make them famous in the BASE community. Since many BASE jumps are breaking rules or laws, it's not always easy to get "official" records. There's no "BASE Jumping League" to check out every story. (There is a ProBASE World Cup, however. Jumpers aim for perfect landings or they get points for doing acrobatics during their short jumps.)

Here are stories of some of the most thrilling and amazing BASE jumps and jumpers.

- Phil Smith became the first person to officially jump off each of the four BASE jumps. When he soared off a building in Houston, Texas, in 1981, he earned his last letter—B. He also became BASE No. 1. That numbering system continues today. Each person who completes the BASE gets a number. There are more than 2,000 people who have earned a BASE number.

- The two men from Chapter 1— Al Neyadi and Omar Al Hegelan—set the record for highest jump from a building . . . a record that can't be topped until someone builds a taller building!

- In 1992, a pair of Australians leaped off the Trango Tower in Pakistan. This enormous rock face looms more than 20,600 feet (6,286 meters) above the ground!

Record setters look for tall towers like this one.

The Snake River flows beneath this famous jumping bridge in Idaho.

- While those jumps gained glory for one person each, other BASE jump events aim for different records. In 2010, 25 people jumped off the Perrine Bridge (also called Potato Bridge) over the Snake River in Idaho. The bridge is one of the few places in the United States where BASE jumping is fully legal.

Some jumpers aim for quantity. Miles Daisher claims to have made more BASE jumps than anyone, with more than 2,500 to his credit. He also holds the unofficial record for most BASE jumps in one day. He had help packing his chutes, but he had to hike to the top of the cliff he was jumping from.

Finally, while jumping from a high place is BASE jumper heaven . . . jumping from a really low place is also very cool for them. They have to pop their chute immediately and hope they can slow down enough before the ground arrives to meet them. In 1990, a British man named Russell Powell jumped inside St. Paul's Cathedral in London. The walkway he jumped from was only 225 feet (68.5 m) above the ground!

BASE jumping thrills some daring jumpers . . . but it scares the daylights out of the rest of us!

Indoors? You can just see jumper Russell Powell
as he comes down in a church in London.

Glossary

daredevil—a person who takes extreme physical risks

fatal—causing death

lofty—very high up

plummeted—fell very quickly from a height

reputation—what other people think about you

Find Out More

BOOKS

Extreme Skydiving
By Bobbie Kalman. New York, NY: Crabtree, 2006.
BASE jumping is just one of the amazing ways that people dive through the air. This book includes information on skysurfing, group skydiving, and other high-flying action sports.

WEB SITES

For links to learn more about extreme sports: **childsworld.com/links**

Note to Parents, Teachers, and Librarians: We routinely verify our Web links to make sure they are safe and active sites. So encourage your readers to check them out!

Index

About the Author

K. C. Kelley is way too afraid of heights to consider doing any BASE jumping. He's much happier staying in his office and writing sports and adventure books for young readers.